GW00732794

DISCOVER
OCEANS

Predominant artwork & imagery source:
Shutterstock.com
Copyright: North Parade Publishing Ltd.
3-6 Henrietta Mews,
Bath.
BA2 6LR.UK

This edition: 2022

All rights reserved. No part of this publication
may be reprinted, stored in a retrieval system
or transmitted, in any form or by any means,
electronic, mechanical, photocopying, recording,
or otherwise, without the prior permission of the
copyright holder.

Printed in China.

CONTENTS

INTRODUCTION

There is a reason why you won't find boundaries for the five oceans in the planet. The ocean is one large body of water covering Earth and giving the planet its characteristic vibrant blue colour. Surrounded by continents, this massive ocean is divided into five regions. In the order of size, they are: Pacific, Atlantic, Indian, Arctic and Antarctic or Southern Oceans.

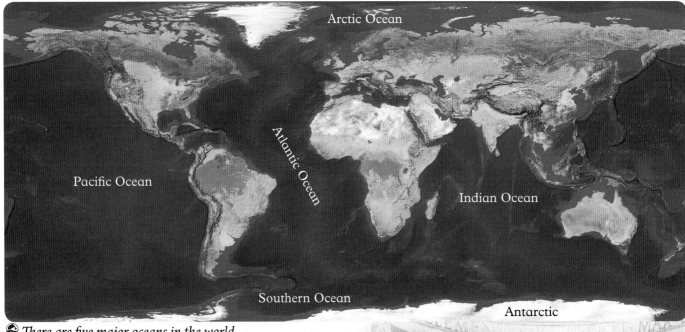

Arctic Ocean

Atlantic Ocean

Pacific Ocean

Indian Ocean

Southern Ocean

Antarctic

🌀 *There are five major oceans in the world*

How was the Ocean Formed?

The ocean appeared millions of years ago when the planet finally cooled down. Several layers of rock accumulated and volcanic eruptions were frequent. Large amounts of steam ejected from the volcanoes collected in the atmosphere to form water vapour. They condensed to form rain. The rain fell for thousands of years to create the depressions that formed the first seas.

The word 'ocean' is derived from the Greek word *Oceanus* referring to a Greek figure personifying the seas. The oceans constitute the major portion of Earth, covering nearly 70% of the surface. The oceanic waters are so deep that they hide massive mountains, active volcanoes and deep trenches. These underwater oceanic landscapes are constantly in the process of change.

The old crust is pushed into the mantle and replaced by new crust forming along the mid-oceanic ridges. We know that this phenomenon occurs because the oldest oceanic rocks date back only 200 million years. Since we know that the Earth formed nearly 4.5 billion years ago, the only explanation is that a new crust arises periodically through the ridge to replace the old one.

🌀 *Oceanus, the namesake of oceans*

The underwater volcanoes and hydrothermal vents provided the right environment for life to originate. Much later, primitive organisms began to evolve and over millions of years, more complex organisms also evolved. The fossils of ancient marine creatures give us valuable information about the conditions prevailing at that time.

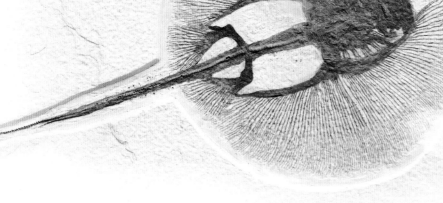

🌀 *Fossil remains of ancient marine creatures preserved in rock*

Fact File

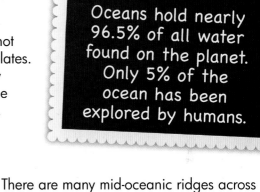

Oceans hold nearly 96.5% of all water found on the planet. Only 5% of the ocean has been explored by humans.

Mid-Oceanic System

A mid-oceanic ridge is a mountain range deep under the ocean formed by plate tectonics. The outermost crust layer of the Earth is not continuous; it is made up of small and big fragments, also called plates. They are constantly in motion, gliding over the mantle layer directly beneath them. This is known as plate tectonics. The movement of the plates is powered by the convection currents rising from the mantle.

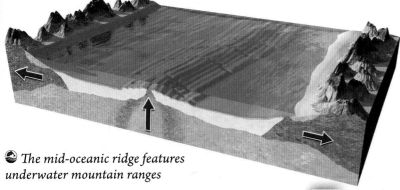

🌀 *The mid-oceanic ridge features underwater mountain ranges*

There are many mid-oceanic ridges across the Earth's surface. They are all connected and form one massive mid-oceanic ridge system across all five oceans. The mid-oceanic system is the longest mountain range in the world, with a total length of nearly 60,000 kilometres!

Oceans and Weather

The oceans are not only home to thousands of species, but also vital for shaping our planet's climate and weather patterns. Of the sunlight striking Earth, more than 50% is absorbed by the oceans. When the ocean water turns warm, it provides the energy needed to drive storms. Rain from storms provides freshwater vital for living organisms. Oceans also moderate temperatures along the coasts.

🌀 *The ocean currents regulate temperature and weather patterns*

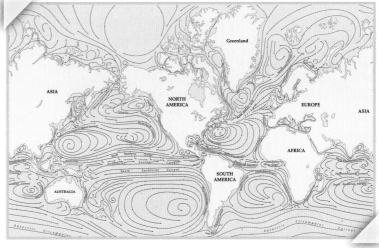

Among the five oceans, the Pacific Ocean is not only the largest but also the deepest. It covers about a third of the Earth's surface and covers an area larger than all the continents combined together. Followed by it are the Atlantic Ocean and Indian Ocean. These oceans are important in maintaining life and regulating climate. They also face the same issues such as oil pollution, overfishing and endangered marine species.

North Pacific Ocean

South Pacific Ocean

The Pacific Ocean is massive and borders four continents

The Pacific Ocean

The word 'Pacific' is borrowed from a Latin word which means 'peaceful'. It was the Portuguese explorer, Ferdinand Magellan who first called the waters 'mar pacifico' which means 'peaceful sea'. However, it is here that some of the most powerful storms in the world brew.

Ferdinand Magellan, a Portuguese explorer, called the ocean 'mar pacifico'

There are many islands dotting the Pacific Ocean

The Pacific Ocean extends all the way from the Arctic Ocean in the north down to Antarctica in the south. The ocean is dotted with thousands of small volcanic islands such as Hawaii, Samoa and Tonga. Indonesia alone is made up of 17,508 islands. A volcanically active region called the 'Ring of Fire' is located in this ocean. The Great Barrier Reef, the largest structure made up of living organisms, is also found in the Pacific Ocean. The Pacific Ocean borders four continents: North America, South America, Asia and Australia.

The Atlantic Ocean

Roughly covering 25% of the Earth's surface, the Atlantic Ocean is named after Atlas in Greek mythology and means 'Sea of Atlas'. It is believed to have formed during the Jurassic period, about 150 million years ago. Among the five oceans, the Atlantic Ocean has the highest level of salinity.

The Mid-Atlantic Ridge runs roughly from Iceland to Argentina. The most well-known waterway in the Atlantic Ocean is the Straits of Gibraltar between Morocco and Spain. It is the first ocean that was crossed by ship or plane.

North Atlantic Ocean

South Atlantic Ocean

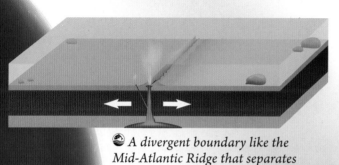

🌊 *A divergent boundary like the Mid-Atlantic Ridge that separates Eurasia from North America*

🌊 *The Atlantic Ocean is named in honor of a Greek titan, Atlas*

The Indian Ocean

This ocean is located between Africa on the west and Australia and Asia on the east. It is called the Indian Ocean because it is located in the Indian peninsula. It is the warmest among the five oceans, but due to its low oxygen levels, it does not support as many living species as other oceans. The total area that the Indian Ocean covers is approximately 28,350,000 square miles. In terms of size, the Indian Ocean is world's third-largest ocean. The two that are bigger than the Indian Ocean are the Atlantic Ocean and the Pacific Ocean.

🌊 *The Indian Ocean is the third-largest ocean*

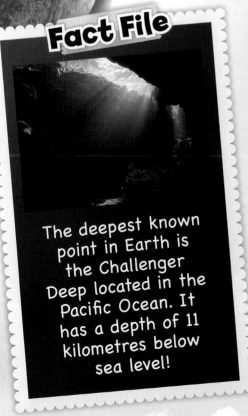

Fact File

The deepest known point in Earth is the Challenger Deep located in the Pacific Ocean. It has a depth of 11 kilometres below sea level!

Indian Ocean

THE ARCTIC AND THE SOUTHERN OCEANS

The Arctic Ocean, located in the North Pole, and the Southern Ocean, surrounding Antarctica in the south, make up the two other major oceans. One of the most prominent features of both these oceans is the obvious water temperature. While the other oceans are moderately warm, both these oceans have an average temperature below freezing point at around -2°C

The Arctic Ocean

The Arctic Ocean is the smallest among the five oceans and also the one with the shallowest waters. It is located in the northern hemisphere and surrounded by North America and Eurasia. Throughout the winter, the ocean is almost completely covered in ice. Even during the warmer months, it is at least partially covered in ice. Fridtjof Nansen was one of the first people to cross the Arctic Ocean in 1896.

Arctic Ocean

The ocean is roughly the same size of Russia. The North Pole is located in the middle of the Arctic Ocean.

🌀 *Fridtjof Nansen led an expedition to cross the Arctic Ocean*

🌀 *The Arctic Ocean is the smallest among the five oceans*

Different Types of Ice

The Arctic Ocean is almost always covered in ice, but it's not the same ice everywhere. There are three types of ice cover: polar ice, pack ice and fast ice. Polar ice does not melt and can be about 2 metres in thickness in summer, while during the winter it can be about 50 metres thick! The ice located around the edges of polar ice is called pack ice. This type of ice freezes only during the cold winter months. Fast ice forms during the winter around the existing pack ice and land area.

🌀 *Fast ice forms on existing pack ice*

Life in and around the Arctic Ocean

A wide range of marine species survive in the cold waters of the Arctic Ocean. They include fish, seals, whales, walruses and jellyfish. There are more fish species found in the Arctic Ocean than anywhere else.

Polar bears live and hunt along the coast of the ocean. The ocean and the region derive their name from the Greek word 'arktos' which means 'bear'. This refers to the great bear and little bear constellations that can be observed here. The Arctic Ocean is currently covered by an ice cap, but it is rapidly melting and disintegrating. If global warming continues, there will be no ice cap left in the Arctic Ocean and this will directly affect the survival of polar bears.

Fact File

The famous ship Titanic sank after hitting an iceberg that originally broke away from a glacier in the Arctic Ocean.

Melting ice in the Arctic region affects polar bears

The Southern Ocean

The waters of the other four oceans meet around Antarctica and are called the Southern Ocean or the Antarctic Ocean. It is the fourth largest; bigger than the Arctic Ocean. Part of the ocean freezes during the extremely cold winters. The powerful winds in the Antarctic region make the waters very choppy and difficult for sailors to navigate. The Southern Ocean is the only ocean that reaches all the way around the globe. It is here that some of the largest and tallest icebergs are found. B-15, measuring 295 kilometres in length, was the largest recorded iceberg, that broke off from the Ross Ice Shelf in Antarctica.

Several icebergs are found in the Southern Ocean

OCEAN ZONES

The ocean is teeming with life right from the surface to the deep seafloor. Ranging from microscopic plankton to mighty whales, the ocean is a rich ecosystem that is still largely undiscovered. The ocean is divided into five major zones, each inhabited by organisms adapted for survival there.

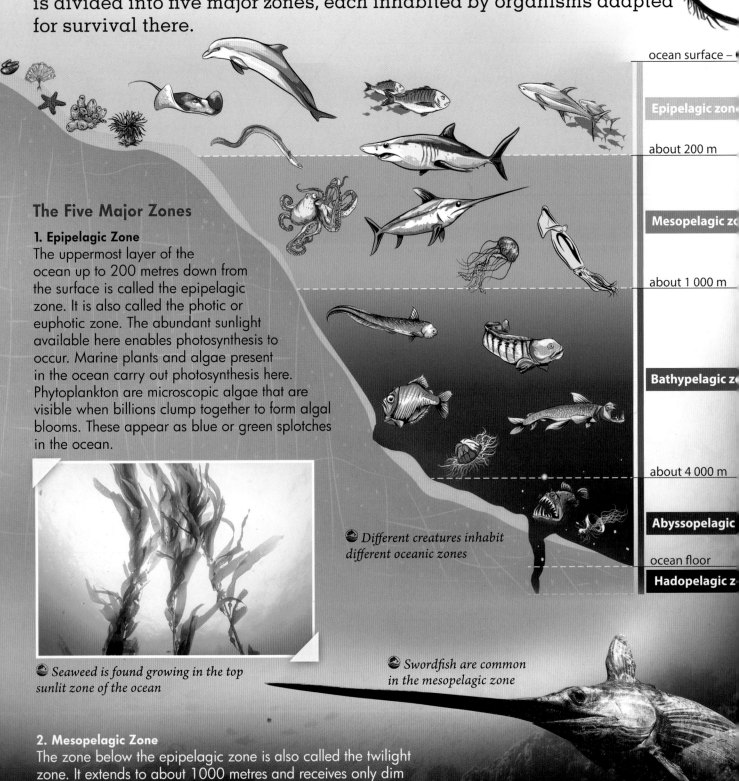

ocean surface –

Epipelagic zone

about 200 m

Mesopelagic zone

about 1 000 m

Bathypelagic zone

about 4 000 m

Abyssopelagic

ocean floor

Hadopelagic zone

🌀 *Different creatures inhabit different oceanic zones*

The Five Major Zones

1. Epipelagic Zone

The uppermost layer of the ocean up to 200 metres down from the surface is called the epipelagic zone. It is also called the photic or euphotic zone. The abundant sunlight available here enables photosynthesis to occur. Marine plants and algae present in the ocean carry out photosynthesis here. Phytoplankton are microscopic algae that are visible when billions clump together to form algal blooms. These appear as blue or green splotches in the ocean.

🌀 *Seaweed is found growing in the top sunlit zone of the ocean*

🌀 *Swordfish are common in the mesopelagic zone*

2. Mesopelagic Zone

The zone below the epipelagic zone is also called the twilight zone. It extends to about 1000 metres and receives only dim sunlight. While there are no marine plants or algae here, large fish species and whales hunt in this zone for food. The fish found here are often small in size and capable of luminosity. Wolf eel and swordfish are common species found in the mesopelagic zone.

🐚 *The pelican eel is so named because its mouth resembles a pelican's beak*

3. Bathypelagic Zone

Below the mesopelagic zone is a region of no sunlight, extending to about 4000 metres. It is also known as the midnight zone. The fauna found in this zone have certain characteristic features: poor eyesight, small mouth, strong gills, sharp teeth and expandable stomach. Food is rare in this zone, and the dwellers rely on remains of plants and animals that come down from the zones above. The pelican eel is one of the species that live here.

4. Abyssopelagic Zone

This zone includes the region at the bottom of the ocean with an average temperature of 2°C. The depth of this zone extends up to 6000 metres. The pressure is very high here, and it is impossible for most life-forms to survive. Those marine organisms that dwell in this zone have adaptations that allow them to survive in high pressure with minimal food availability. The few fish species living here have wide jaws that look almost unhinged. This allows them to drag their open mouth across the floor to find any food available. Bioluminescent squid and fish live here. The anglerfish has a glowing light extending out from its head to attract prey.

Fact File

Phytoplankton and seaweed produce nearly 70% of the world's oxygen through photosynthesis.

🐚 *Creatures in this zone, like the anglerfish, exhibit bioluminescence*

🐚 *Amphipods thrive in the extreme conditions of the hadopelagic zone*

5. Hadopelagic Zone

This is the deepest zone in the ocean, found in trenches and canyons underwater. Very few organisms live here. Those that do survive on dead or decaying plant and animal matter (marine detritus). A few creatures feed on bacteria found around hydrothermal vents that ooze out nutrient-rich minerals from the Earth's interior. Bristle worms, bivalves, amphipods and gastropods dwell here.

DEEP SEA DWELLERS

Creatures living several hundred metres below the sea are equipped with special adaptations to help them survive. The abyssopelagic zone is one of the most food-limited environments among all ocean zones. Since this zone still remains vastly unexplored, we know only a few of the many species living here.

Vampire Squid: Living 3000 metres below the surface, the vampire squid has the largest eyes proportional to the body among all animals. It has webbed arms that it wraps around itself like a cloak. This squid is well-adapted for surviving in the low-oxygen world at the bottom of the oceans.

A vampire squid has a distinct cloak-like covering

Sea cucumbers are commonly found on seafloors across the world

A Sea sponge is made up of pores and channels

Sea sponge: A sea sponge is a basic multicellular organism with a body containing pores and channels. The channels are made up of cells that pump water and food particles.

Sea cucumber: This deep sea creature has an elongated body with the thickness of a cucumber and a leathery skin. Sea cucumbers are found dwelling on seafloors across the world. A sea cucumber's mouth is surrounded by tentacles which open to feed on floating plankton and decaying matter at the bottom. Sea cucumbers form large herds that move together to scavenge for food.

If the cells of the sponge's body are broken apart, they can reattach to form new sponges—something that no other known creature can achieve!

🌊 *The viperfish's teeth are its prominent feature*

Viperfish: One of the most unusual fish species discovered, the viperfish has large teeth to hold on to prey. Living at a depth of 1500 to 2800 metres, it produces light to attract prey. It has a low metabolic rate which enables it to go for days without food. While it generally lives for 15 – 30 years in the ocean, in captivity, it lasts for only a few hours.

🌊 *The frilled shark gets its name from the frilly appearance of its gill slits*

Frilled shark: Earning its name from the fluffy appearance of its gills, the frilled shark is very different from other shark species. Living at depths of 1200 – 1500 metres, it is adapted for survival in the abyssal zone of the ocean. It has 200 sharp teeth that it uses to grab prey. It can swallow a creature nearly half its size.

Giant tube worm: These creatures live near hydrothermal vents and eat the bacteria present there. Larval worms have stomachs to ingest as much bacteria as possible to feed them for the rest of their lives. Later, they attach to the ocean floor and develop a hard exoskeleton. Afterwards, they do not have to eat ever again.

🌊 *Giant tube worms attach themselves near vents and feed on bacteria*

MICROSCOPIC MARINE LIFE

Millions of microscopic bacteria, plants and animals make up the major portion of the ocean. Some float on the surface, while others make their living around hydrothermal vents or seafloors. All microscopic organisms in the ocean, even viruses, are important. They help maintain the balance of chemical components and gases for sustaining all life-forms.

Blue-Green Algae and Photosynthesis

Blue-green algae, despite its name, is a type of bacterial species. However, like algae, it possesses chloroplasts for photosynthesis. Also called cyanobacteria, this bacterial species produces oxygen as a by-product of photosynthesis. It lives in colonies on the surface of oceans and contributes to the oxygen needs of hundreds of land and marine species.

🌀 *Excessive growth of blue-green algae is called 'algal bloom'*

Fact File

Dinoflagellates are responsible for the red tides found sometimes in the oceans. The red tide introduces toxins in the water and causes poisoning of fish and shellfish species.

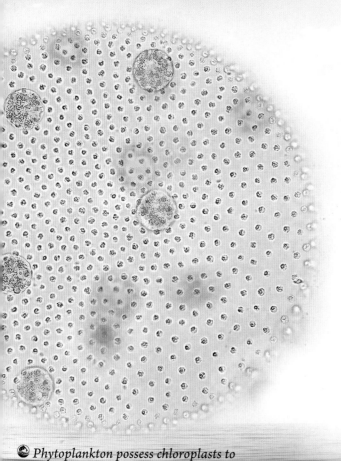

Plankton: The Ocean Wanderers

The ocean has millions of tiny plants and animals floating in its waters. Collectively, they are called plankton. The word 'plankton' is derived from the Greek word which means 'wanderer'. The tiny plants are called phytoplankton while the animals are called zooplankton.

Phytoplankton mostly live on the top layer harvesting sunlight for photosynthesis. They supply nearly 80% of all the oxygen in the oceans. Diatoms are the most common among phytoplanktons.

Zooplankton feed on the phytoplankton for survival. Radiolarians and dinoflagellates are the most common types of zooplankton. Plankton mostly stays afloat drifting along with the tides as they are not equipped for swimming. Diatoms produce oil, which helps keep them afloat in the ocean, while radiolarians have spikes that slow down sinking.

Phytoplankton possess chloroplasts to perform photosynthesis

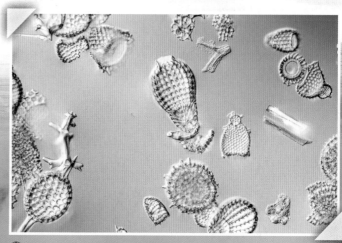

Radiolarians are a common type of zooplankton found in the ocean

Viruses in the Oceans

Viruses are abundant in the oceans. There are more viruses in the ocean than all living cells combined. There are viruses of different kinds capable of infecting every organism, ranging from the tiny bacteria to the mighty whale. Even though viruses primarily kill different hosts they infect, they are still important for maintaining the balance of marine life in the oceans.

Archaea: Survivors from Ancient Times

The archaea are not only the oldest class of microbes to survive on Earth, but also the most abundantly found on the planet. They are important for playing a vital role in recycling different important constituents that sustain life on Earth. They have adapted to survive in different parts of the planet, even under extreme temperature and pressure conditions, as found on the ocean floor around hydrothermal vents. With sunlight absent at the bottom of the ocean, archaea depend on methane and hydrogen sulfide leaching out from the vents, converting them into organic compounds that support several other organisms.

Archaea are found thriving around underwater hydrothermal vents

CRUSTACEANS

The crustaceans are a group of animals with a tough skin, gills, and antennae. Some of the best known among them include crabs, barnacles, krill, lobsters, shrimps, and prawns. Owing to their striking resemblance to insects, they are sometimes referred to as the 'insects of the sea'.

Crustacean Features

Crustaceans have certain distinct features; the most noticeable of them is the tough exoskeleton covering the body. The exoskeleton is made of chitin and proteins. Apart from forming a protective shell, it also protects the animal from drying out. The period when a crustacean sheds its old exoskeleton and produces a new one leaves it vulnerable to attack from predators. Apart from the exoskeleton, a marine crustacean has compound eyes, a well-built head, gills, sensitive antennae, and a segmented body.

Crabs and other crustaceans have a tough exoskeleton

Pistol Shrimp

Also called the snapping shrimp, this remarkable creature might be small, at merely 4 centimetres, but it can make an enormous noise. It has an enlarged claw that it can open and shut with violent force, firing bubbles underwater with such force that it can stun or even kill the prey. Despite its powerful weapon, the shrimp is still exposed to many predators and often lives in large colonies.

The pistol shrimp's weapon is its powerful claw

Arrow Crab

The crab gets its name from the shape of its body, which is triangular and resembles an arrowhead. The crab's long legs also make it similar to a spider. It can grow to a length of about six inches. The arrow crab has a rather bizarre choice of diet – it uses its powerful claws to pull feather duster worms out of their tubes to eat them.

An arrow crab has long, spindly legs

Fact File

The pistol shrimp strikes its claw to shoot bubbles at a predator. The sound produced is much louder than the firing of a gun at 210 decibels!

Furry Lobster

While fur is not common among creatures in the deep sea, the furry lobster is unique. It is covered in short hair all over its body and has long antennae like all lobster species. Three species of furry lobsters have been discovered in shallow waters of different oceans. Interestingly, a furry lobster does not get itself caught in traps set for crayfish or lobsters. It hunts in the night and devours small crabs, mussels, clams and even other lobsters.

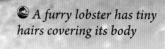
A furry lobster has tiny hairs covering its body

Hermit Crab

The hermit crab has a unique appearance, as it carries its home on its back wherever it goes. The crab's stomach is soft and vulnerable, so it protects itself by inhabiting an empty sea-snail shell. When the hermit crab grows, it abandons the old shell to find a new one. As scavengers, they will eat anything they find in the water.

The hermit crab carries its protective shell everywhere

Cleaner Shrimp

The cleaner shrimp exhibits a very interesting behavior. It helps clean parasites from the damaged scales and mouths of moray eels, groupers and many species of fish. Even though the shrimp could easily be a meal for any of these creatures, they don't eat the shrimp. It cleans inside a fish's mouth in complete safety. The shrimp gains nutrition from the mucus and parasites that it consumes.

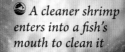
A cleaner shrimp enters into a fish's mouth to clean it

Hundreds of barnacles sticking to a log of wood

Common Barnacle

Barnacles are common in all oceans and frequently occur in clusters. Sometimes, they stick to the underside of boats, docks, drifting wood and even whales. Barnacles feed on plankton and floating debris in the ocean. They spend their entire lives attached permanently to a spot unlike other crustaceans that travel around for food or safety.

SMALL MARINE CREATURES

Beneath the ocean's surface lies a bustling world of marine life hosting many different sizes, colours, shapes and unique features. The different species of individual marine organisms exhibit vast differences in features, external appearance and adaptations.

Cuttlefish

A cuttlefish is an interesting creature best known for its camouflaging ability. Even though several other animals can do this, a cuttlefish can not only change the colour on its skin but also pattern and even texture. Despite its name, a cuttlefish is not a fish; it is a type of mollusk. A mollusk has a soft body without a backbone and possesses arms or tentacles. Found in oceans all over the world, they have a relatively short lifespan of about three years.

A cuttlefish is an expert in camouflage

A sea pen is usually attached to the ocean floor

Fact File

Even though most species of starfish have five arms, there are others that have as many as 40 arms!

Sea Pen

The sea pen is so called owing to its resemblance to the quill used as writing equipment in the olden days. Sea pens are actually a colony of tentacle polyps that are attached to the seafloor. They form branches in deep waters that are not turbulent. Some sea pens exhibit bioluminescence – they emit greenish-blue light when touched. Occasionally, sea pens detach and travel with the currents to relocate to a different place.

There are over 1500 species of starfish across the oceans in the world. They are found everywhere from the seashore to abyssal depths. The upper side of a starfish is brightly coloured and usually covered in plates or spines. A starfish can regenerate broken arms or damaged parts. One species of starfish, the crown-of-thorns starfish, is one of the biggest predators of coral. It has such a disastrous effect on the coral population that it is listed in the top 100 most invasive species in the world.

The crown-of-thorns starfish is a strongly invasive species that feeds on coral

Jellyfish

Also called 'sea jellies', these are free-swimming creatures that have an umbrella-shaped bell and trailing tentacles. The tentacles contain stinging cells that help catch prey as well as attack predators. They do not belong to the fish family. Jellyfish are invertebrates that have either transparent or colourful and sometimes even luminescent bodies. Jellyfish eat their meals very quickly, as the weight of any undigested food hampers their floating ability.

Jellyfish come in a variety of colours

Sea Urchin

A sea urchin is round and spiky and lives at the bottom of the ocean in deep as well as shallow waters. Sea urchins possess spines that can be soft and flexible or hard and spiny. There are more than 200 different species of sea urchins. The spherical shape helps them move around in search of food or to escape from predators. They are found in the oceans all over the world except the polar regions.

Sea urchins are spiny creatures related to starfish

SQUID, OCTOPUSES AND TROPICAL FISH

Fish are an integral part of the ocean and over 14,000 species inhabit the waters at various depths. Squid and octopuses are classified as cephalopods and have distinct heads and eight arms paired into two sets. While octopuses and squid are not as diverse as fish, there are still hundreds of species combined.

A giant squid can measure nearly 14 metres

Fact File

Owing to its size, the only known predator of the giant squid is the giant sperm whale.

Squid

A squid has a soft, tube-shaped body with a short head. It also has a shell that protects the body from the inside. Squid are closely related to octopuses, but have two long tentacles as well as eight arms. The largest of the squid species, the giant squid, is about 14 metres in length and weighs over 100 pounds. The eye of a giant squid is about the same size as a basketball. Squid have suckers at the end of their long arms which helps them catch fish and shellfish.

Octopus

An octopus has a soft, bag-like body, large eyes, and eight arms. Octopuses grow, mature and die quickly. The lifespan of an octopus is only about two to five years. In fact, while a male octopus dies soon after mating, a female octopus lives only long enough to lay eggs, and tend them until they hatch. An octopus has many techniques to escape from predators. It can cleverly camouflage itself to blend into its surroundings. Almost all species are venomous, though only the blue-ringed octopus is dangerous to humans.

Octopuses live only long enough to reproduce

Tropical Fish

There are thousands of colourful fish species of all shapes and sizes adapted for life in the oceans. Small fish typically move together in groups, also called 'schools'. Other fish exist solitarily. Fish have different adaptations depending on their habitat to help them survive.

Oarfish: This is a very long fish that can grow to a length of up to 15 metres. It is considered to be the longest bony fish in the world. Despite its length, it is incredibly thin and can weigh up to 600 pounds. The giant oarfish is also known as the 'king of herrings'.

An oarfish is long and thin

Puffer fish: This fish lives in the well-lit top zone of the ocean and is also known as a blowfish. The reason for its name is its ability to blow itself up into a ball to look more aggressive. This defence mechanism is necessary for the fish as it is a slow swimmer and very susceptible to attack.

Seahorse: Despite its name, a seahorse is a type of fish capable of swimming upright. It has a curled, prehensile tail that helps it grasp for support. The female seahorse lays the eggs, which the male guards in his pouch until they hatch.

A puffer fish looks intimidating when it is bloated

A male seahorse carrying eggs in its pouch

Clownfish: These attractive fish are aggressive by nature. They often live with anemones, amidst their tentacles. The fish get to eat the remains of an anemone's meal and in return they help to clean the anemone of parasites and dead tentacles. Interestingly, all clownfish are born males and develop into females if the need arises.

A clownfish takes refuge among the tentacles of an anemone

The tripod fish is capable of walking on the seabed

Tripod fish: More popularly known as a 'stilt walker', this is a really unique fish that inhabits the seabed. It lives in a harsh environment where food is scarce. It has three elongated, modified fins on its body that allow it to walk on the ocean floor.

MIGHTY MARINE INHABITANTS

Sharks, whales, dolphins, and porpoises make up the large inhabitants of the oceans. Whales, dolphins, and porpoises constitute one family of marine animals called Cetacea. Sharks are large, bony fish that are not only some of the oldest animals still surviving but also the fastest-swimming on the planet.

Killer whales are also called orcas

Sharks

Sharks are fierce predatory fishes that have a skeleton instead of cartilage. They are closely related to rays and are among the oldest animals on the planet. The first sharks are believed to have evolved nearly 300 million years ago. There are over 300 species of sharks, with the whale shark being the largest living fish. A typical whale shark can reach a length of up to 15 metres. At the other end of the spectrum, the dwarf lantern shark is the smallest, measuring just 19 centimetres in length.

The most prominent feature of a shark is its pointed snout, tough skin and rows of sharp teeth. The exception is the hammerhead shark, which has a wide, flat head with a hammer-like projection. Sharks also have muscular tails and pointed fins. Among the sharks, only a few species—including mako shark, tiger shark and white shark—have large teeth.

The great white shark is a fierce predator

The hammerhead shark doesn't have a pointed snout like other species

Sharks hunt by circling their prey and approaching it from below. When a shark smells blood, it enters into a feeding frenzy, attacking and feeding on everything in its path.

Whales

Whales are large animals that resemble fish but are mammals, that is, they give birth to live young and feed them milk. There are many types of whales, though they all come under two basic categories: toothed and baleen.

Toothed whales have sharp teeth and their main diet consists of fish and squid. There are 70 known species of toothed whales. Killer whales, beluga whales, pilot whales, narwhals, dolphins and porpoises are all members of this group.

Baleen whales have no teeth. Instead, they have blade-like plates hanging from the roof of their mouths. These plates are called 'baleen'. They are also sometimes referred to as whalebones. Without teeth, these whales do not hunt for prey like sharks do. Instead, the whale feeds by swimming with its mouth open and gulps water. The inner side of a baleen whale's mouth has bristles to trap food. The baleen acts as a filter retaining shrimp, fish and plankton.

Fact File

Sharks are constantly losing and replacing teeth. In its lifetime, a shark can grow thousands of teeth.

The baleen plates filter food for the whale

Whales grow to lengths of 3 to 18 metres depending on the species. There are 10 known species of baleen whales. The blue whale is the largest animal in the world and can reach a total length of nearly 30 metres.

Whales need to go to the surface to breathe. A whale takes in enough air through blowholes located on top of its head before diving in. A whale has smooth skin with a layer of fat called blubber underneath for protection from the cold water.

Dolphins and porpoises have distinct features

Dolphins and Porpoises

Dolphins and porpoises are intelligent mammals and communicate through a bulb-like structure on the front of their heads. A dolphin is very distinct from a porpoise. While a dolphin has an elongated snout, the porpoise's snout is squat. Dolphins have cone-shaped teeth while those of porpoises are shovel-shaped. Dolphins have hook-shaped fins, different from the triangular fins of porpoises. A dolphin can make a whistling sound that a porpoise is incapable of producing.

CORAL REEFS

A coral reef is a large marine ecosystem that exists underwater. It is made up of colonies of marine invertebrates, called corals. Coral reefs look like rocks, but they are made up of the deposits of calcium carbonate secreted by corals. They are found all over the world, but the biggest reefs are found in tropical and subtropical shallow waters.

Reef Formation

Many of the coral reefs found around the world are several thousand years old. They grow in regions with plenty of sunshine to allow algae to flourish. It is algae that act as the major food source for the corals.

The coral reefs constitute merely 1% of the ocean floor yet they are among the most diverse and productive ecosystems on this planet. Nearly 25% of all known marine species rely on coral reefs for shelter, food and reproduction. This includes over 4000 species of fish, 700 different species of coral and thousands of other marine flora and fauna. Not surprisingly, coral reefs are called the 'rainforests of the sea'. Coral reefs are classified into three types based on its location. The inner reef is located close to the shore. The outer reef or fore reef is farthest from the shore. Between these two is found the reef crest.

An atoll is found in the middle of the ocean

There are four different types of coral reef formations:

Atoll: It is a ring-like structure forming a protected lagoon in the middle of an ocean around partially or fully sunk islands.

Fringing: It is the most common type of reef growing very close to the coastline.

Barrier: A barrier reef is separated from the coastline by deep and wide lagoons.

Patch: It grows between a barrier reef and fringing reef on an island or continental shelf.

Coral reefs are colourful and a major source of attraction for tourists

Threats to Coral Reefs

Coral reefs are not only a source of beauty but also a protective barrier against erosion of coastlines. In recent decades, coral reefs have been facing destruction. Since they take a long time to form but disintegrate quickly, they are at risk of being wiped out completely. Most of the damage inflicted on coral reefs is being caused by humans, directly or indirectly, through different activities.

There are different factors that pose a threat to coral reefs. They include:

Climate change: Corals have survived for thousands of years, but are threatened with extinction today due to higher water temperature, among other causes. Global warming has taken a severe toll on the reefs. Coral reefs are gradually getting bleached or turning white. Coral bleaching occurs when the water is too warm or saline and the algae die out.

Destructive fishing and overfishing: Using dynamite, cyanide and bottom trawling to harvest fish causes profound damage to the coral reefs: toppling their ecosystem balance.

Careless tourists: Even tourism can affect coral reefs when the boats bump against the reefs or if tourists touch or step on them. Certain resorts are built directly on top of reefs while others empty sewage in the water around the reefs.

Pollution: Ranging from oil spillage to industrial waste effluent, all chemical substances disturb the balance of chemical components in the water and wreak havoc.

Aerial view of the Great Barrier Reef

The Great Barrier Reef

The Great Barrier Reef is the largest reef system in the planet. It is made up of more than 3000 individual reefs and coral cays. The reef supports hundreds of species ranging from tiny plankton to massive whales.

It is located off the east coast of Queensland, Australia, and stretches for about 2000 kilometres. The reef is home to over 2000 fish species, 4000 molluscs, and 250 species of shrimp.

Even the corals that make up the reef exhibit immense variety, with nearly 400 species of coral making up this gigantic structure. Since the reef is located in tropical water, where it is warm enough for swimming and diving, it attracts a lot of tourists. The Great Barrier Reef was declared as a World Heritage Site in 1981.

Fact File

Coral reefs form very slowly. Growing at a rate of merely 1 to 2 centimetres per year, many of the large reefs present today took thousands of years to form.

OCEANIC TIDES AND TIDE POWER

Oceanic tides are produced by the cyclic rise and fall of water in the seas and oceans. The major factor driving tides is the gravitation attraction between the Earth and the Moon. The power of the tides can be harnessed to produce a clean and renewable energy called tidal energy.

The Tide Controllers

The Moon is the major factor that controls the rhythm as well as the height of tides. The gravitational attraction between the Earth and Moon creates two tidal bulges. The tidal bulge closest to the Moon is drawn towards it and is of greater strength, while the bulge on the opposite side is weaker.

Apart from the Moon, the Sun also plays a role in controlling tides. Even though the massive Sun can exert a higher gravitational pull, the distance between the Sun and Earth restricts the strength. So, the Sun's gravitational force on Earth is only about 46% that of the Moon. When the Sun's gravitational pull combines with that of the Moon's, it can create significant tidal variation.

Earth

Moon

gravitational force
of the Moon

high tide   high tide

Tides are caused by Moon's gravitational pull

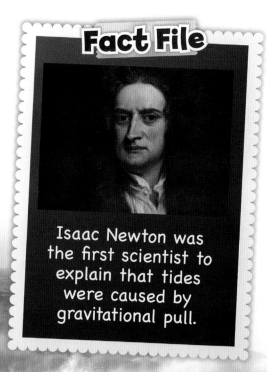
Fact File

Isaac Newton was the first scientist to explain that tides were caused by gravitational pull.

Tide Cycles

The tides change based on the Moon's rotation around the Earth as well as the change in position of the Sun. Throughout the day, the sea level continues to rise and fall. The cycle occurs once or twice every day depending on the location with respect to the Moon. Tides that cycle once a day are called diurnal while those that cycle twice a day are called semidiurnal. The rise and fall of sea levels results in water flowing in and out of the ocean resulting in the formation of currents called tidal currents. They are primarily of three types:

Flood: This occurs when the sea level rises and water is flowing away from the ocean and towards the shore.

Ebb: It is caused by a dip in sea level, and water retreats from the shore towards the ocean.

Slack water: At the exact point of high or low tide, there is no current and this is referred to as slack water.

Water swells towards the shore

A tidal power station produces tidal energy similar to a hydroelectric station

Tidal Power

The potential energy contained in the ocean water due to the continuous rise and fall of sea levels can be utilized efficiently. The generation of electricity from tides is very similar to generation of hydroelectricity from flowing water. There are different ways through which the power of waves can be harnessed for generating energy.

Reservoirs: They are situated close to the coastline. When water moves into the reservoir and back into the ocean, it is passed through a tube. This tube turns the blades of a turbine that converts the spinning motion into electricity.

Surface devices: These devices are typically held afloat so that they can harvest the power from the up-and-down motion of waves.

Underwater devices: There are different types of underwater devices ranging from balloon-type equipment to tube-like structures. The waves cause them to oscillate and in turn power a turbine that can produce electricity.

TSUNAMIS

A tsunami is a series of massive ocean waves approaching the coast and capable of causing destruction. The surges of water reach heights exceeding 30 metres and are often called 'walls of water'. They crash on the shore and cause widespread damage in the immediate vicinity.

How does a Tsunami Occur?

Tsunamis can be triggered by different physical phenomena like earthquakes, large meteorite impacts, erosion or underwater volcanoes. Large earthquakes occurring under the sea are the most common triggers. These earthquakes occur in the tectonic plate boundaries.

When the ocean floor rises or falls at a plate boundary, it results in the displacement of the water above. The water is launched in the form of rolling waves and gathers force as a tsunami. A tsunami can also be caused by landslides or volcanoes erupting underwater. In the past, meteorite impacts in oceans have caused massive tsunamis.

Nearly 80% of tsunamis occur in a region called the 'Ring of Fire' in the Pacific Ocean. It is a geologically active region where volcanoes and earthquakes occur frequently.

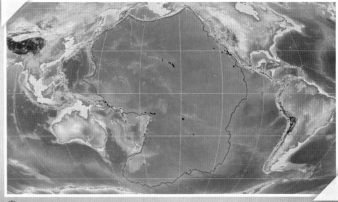
The Ring of Fire is a hot spot for natural calamities

A tsunami travels across the sea at the rate of 805 kilometres per hour – at about the speed of a jet plane. At this speed, it is possible for a tsunami to cover the entire expanse of an ocean in a day. What makes tsunamis powerful is the fact that they lose very little energy on the way.

In the deep ocean, the tsunami waves appear only a few inches high. As they approach the shallow waters of the coast, the waves slow down and grow in height.

A tsunami is characterized by massive surges of water

When a Tsunami Strikes

When a tsunami approaches the coast, it is the lower part, or the trough, that touches the land first. As soon as that happens, it produces a vacuum effect, sucking the coastal water towards the sea. Harbors and seafloors are exposed when this happens. This is an important early indication that a tsunami is about to strike in a few minutes' time. This warning sign can help people staying near the coast to move away to safety.

Warning signs keeps people away from danger-prone areas

Fact File

The top part of the waves move faster than the bottom part and that is the reason why tsunami tides rise precipitously high.

A tsunami does not come as a single giant wave. It is made up of a series of waves, called a wave train. The first wave may not be dangerous nor indicate that the damage is over. A tsunami can typically wreak havoc for several hours before its energy dissipates.

There are several geological structures such as reefs, undersea formations and bays that can dissipate the energy of a tsunami. The flooding caused by a tsunami can extend to about 300 metres or more. The sheer force of these giant waves can tear apart houses, lift boulders and flip vehicles. The word 'tsunami' is a Japanese word which means 'harbor wave'. The best way to evacuate people to safety when a tsunami is approaching is to heed the early warning system. The Pacific Tsunami Warning System is a cooperation of 26 nations with its headquarters in Hawaii. It uses sophisticated seismic equipment to identify tsunamis across different coastal areas around the world.

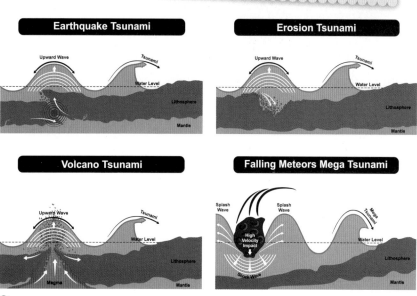

Tsunamis can be triggered by different phenomena

COASTAL LANDSCAPES

Wherever oceans meet continental shores, several coastal landscapes are formed. Some of the most prominent landscapes include reefs, beaches, lagoons, estuaries and islands. Found across the planet, each coastal landscape has its own significance.

An island is surrounded by water on all sides

Island

An island is an area of land considerably smaller than a continent and surrounded on all sides by water. It occurs in oceans, lakes and rivers. A group of islands is known as an archipelago. Islands that emerge from the ocean floor basins are volcanic in nature. The volcanic activity continuously spews out lava that accumulates until it emerges above the surface.

A reef is made up of rocks and sand

Beach

A beach is the land lying along a body of water. The land is typically made up of loose particles of sand, gravel, shingle and pebbles. The waves also deposit biological material including coral algae and shells.

Rocky Reef

Called 'island habitats', reefs are typically rocky regions surrounded by vast areas of sand. Reefs, like the Great Barrier Reef along the coast of Australia, are biological hot spots. They provide a habitat for hundreds of species such as algae, coral, sponges, limpets and urchins. They are also an important nursing and feeding ground for several species of crabs and fish.

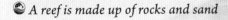

The waves constantly deposit material along the shores

Hawaii is an example of a volcanic island. It is about 9700 metres above the ocean floor!

There's More to a Beach

Did you know that there's more to a beach than what you thought was just sand and sea? The part above the water and the one actively under the influence of waves is called the beach berm. The berm consists of the deposit of various materials and comprises the active and ever-changing shoreline.

The berm, in turn, has three parts: a crest, the top portion; a face, which is the slope leading towards the water from the crest; and a trough, the bottom portion.

Further into the sea, there might be one or more shore bars. A shore bar is a slightly raised, underwater embankment formed at the position where waves first start to break.

An atoll is formed by a ring of coral growing around a submerged island

Lagoon

A lagoon is any body of water separated from the ocean by a natural barrier. The two most common types of lagoons are atolls and coastal lagoons. An atoll forms when an island submerges under the water, leaving behind only a ring of coral that continues to grow upward. The combination of coral growth and the water produces a nearly circular formation. Coastal lagoons form along gently sloping coasts. They are connected to the ocean through inlets between islands.

Estuary

An estuary is a semi-enclosed body of water situated between land and ocean. The water in an estuary is less saline than that of an ocean due to the inflow of freshwater. It is a dynamic ecosystem that supports very high diversity.

An estuary supports several forms of life

ICEBERGS

An iceberg is a chunk of ice that forms on land and then floats into an ocean or a lake. Icebergs can range in size from small 5-metre blocks to ones as large as a small country! They occur only in places where the temperature is cold throughout the year. So, icebergs are typically found in the cold waters surrounding the North Atlantic Ocean and Antarctica.

The part of the iceberg below the water might be larger than what is above

How Do Icebergs Form?

An iceberg forms when chunks of ice calve and break off from massive formations such as glaciers or ice shelves. Icebergs travel in oceans and end up on the shores or get stuck in shallow waters. Greenland and Antarctica are the major sources of the world's largest icebergs.

When an iceberg travels from cold to warm waters, the change in climate has an impact on it. The warm air melts the snow on the surface of the iceberg. The ice melts to form pools called melt ponds. These can, in turn, trickle into the iceberg and widen existing cracks. The warm waters surrounding the iceberg lap around its edges and underneath. This causes the ice to melt and chunks to break off and float away.

Icebergs and Ships

Ever since the disaster inflicted upon the *Titanic*, a British ocean liner traveling to New York, in 1912, ships have been wary of icebergs. Thirteen countries, including the United States, formed an International Ice Patrol to detect icebergs and warn ships in close proximity to the North Atlantic region, where they are common. Most parts of an iceberg are below water, with only as little as an eighth of it being visible. This makes it difficult to assess how problematic it might be and this is the source of the phrase 'tip of the iceberg'.

Iceberg Valley is a location in the northern Atlantic Ocean that is known for its high number of icebergs. It is located about 250 miles away from Newfoundland, Canada. It was here that the *Titanic* sank.

Airplanes and radars are the primary ways for tracking icebergs floating in any of the shipping routes. The U.S. National Ice Center uses data from satellites to observe icebergs larger than 500 square metres, located in the Antarctic region.

Studying Icebergs – Why Is It Important?

Scientists study icebergs because they are useful for understanding ocean processes and climate change. When icebergs break up from the source, they provide vital clues about the underlying causes. Ice shelves disintegrate for various reasons and understanding this can be helpful for predicting patterns in a warmer climate caused by global warming.

Oceanographers are also interested in continuously tracking icebergs as they travel. The freshwater that they contribute to the sea can influence ocean circulation and currents several kilometres away from their origin. Biologists are also interested in knowing how icebergs influence marine life. The nutrients that leach out from icebergs have been found to support plankton, fish and other species.

Icebergs often break off from ice shelves

Fact File

The most dangerous types of icebergs are small in size and hence difficult for ships to spot before it's too late. They are called growlers or bergy bits.

FISHING

Fishing is an important commercial activity carried out for the purpose of food and oil. Even though the amount of fish caught varies, it is roughly estimated to be about 88 million tons per year across the world. Natural causes and human activities are important factors in determining the fish available in the oceans.

Fishing in the Ocean

About 50% of the fish species in the world are found in the oceans and are caught for providing food for humans. Fishing is a major commercial operation that has grown from mere fishing lines and nets to sophisticated technology for mass harvest. Specialized fishing vessels cruise the oceans, catching fish, sorting them on board and bringing them back to the shore.

Since the oceans are vast, it would be natural to assume that the fish present here would be limitless and renewable. However, fisheries are now catching fish faster than the species can renew themselves. Such overfishing can endanger certain species of fish and damage the balance existing in the marine ecosystem.

Massive quantities of fish are caught from the ocean

Fishing Across the World

There are at least 30,000 known species of fish in the world, of which about 500 are edible. Many of the edible species are found in oceans, including salmon, tuna and whitefish. Apart from fish, oysters, clams, crabs, shrimps, prawns and lobsters are also harvested for food.

Different fish species are found in different parts of the ocean. Tuna is found in the open ocean; salmon, whitefish and shrimp occur along the coasts. Clams, oysters and mussels are abundant in estuaries. Many fish species are found in an area called an 'upwelling', where nutrient-rich water supports high productivity. The countries majorly involved in fishing are China, the United States, Chile, Peru, Japan, Indonesia, Thailand, Iceland and Norway.

Fact File

The Atlantic cod is now classified as a vulnerable species, after its population declined in the 1990s due to overfishing.

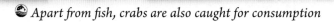
🐟 *Apart from fish, crabs are also caught for consumption*

The Many Methods of Fishing

Fish are caught through different ways. Ranging from casting nets to huge trawlers, different methods are employed to catch many common species. The most popular species include: cod, herring, flounder, tuna, anchovy, shrimp, mullet, salmon, scallops and oyster. Apart from these, crustaceans such as crabs, lobsters and prawn are also highly sought after. Even though most of the fish are caught for food, nearly 40% are used for other purposes such as fishmeal, fish oil, or aquariums. Many are also frozen for future use.

Fishing has increased nearly five-fold in the past five decades. It accounts for 16% of animal protein consumption by humans. This industry directly and indirectly employs 10 million people.

Generally, the fish that are caught are divided into two categories. One pile consists of the fully grown, adult fish and the other pile consists of undersized or diseased fish that are usually thrown back into the ocean. Unintended catches are also released because their absence might cause imbalance in the ecosystems.

🐟 *Fish oil is another major product extracted from species like cod*

OCEAN RESOURCES

The ocean is a valuable source of many useful resources. It provides food in the form of fish and shellfish amounting to millions of pounds each year. Apart from this, the ocean is also important for shipping and travel. Important resources mined from the ocean include minerals, salt, gravel, sand, metals and crude oil.

🌀 *Dredging is employed for finding valuable minerals and gems*

Mining in the Ocean

People began mining the ocean floor for precious metals such as gold, silver, diamond, and other metal ores in the 1950s. Diamonds are of better quality and more abundantly found in the ocean than on land, but it is harder to mine them there. The common method used for finding diamonds is to dredge the ocean floor, bring up the sediment to a boat, and sift through it for gems. The process is difficult because it is not easy to bring up the sediment quickly to the surface.

Hunting for Pearls

Pearl diving is the process of exploring underwater for valuable pearls that are used in ornaments and decorative items.

Before the 20th century, pearl divers descended 100 feet or more on a single breath to hunt for pearls. This was a risky maneuver that exposed them to dangerous marine species and high pressure.

Nowadays, pearl diving has been largely replaced by pearl farms that artificially induce oysters to produce pearls. Through this method, billions of pearls are produced every year, compared to the low yield of the traditional diving. On many coasts, pearling has been prohibited due to the dwindling populations of pearl oysters.

🌀 *Pearls are extracted from oysters and used for making ornaments*

The Mega Climate Buffer

The ocean is one of the vital components of the world's climate because it can collect and drive water, heat and carbon dioxide. It can do it more effectively than the atmosphere. The ocean and atmosphere work together to dictate weather phenomena such as storms and rain across the world. The ocean buffers climate primarily by transporting heat through ocean currents, cooling the tropical regions and warming those higher up in latitude. The average temperature of the planet is maintained at a constant level due to the heat cycled by the oceans.

Hunting for Metals

Metal ores and gravel are commonly mined from the ocean. Manganese nodules that also contained other metals such as nickel, cobalt and copper were first mined from the seafloor in the 1960s. Since then, the oceans have been explored and exploited for metals and minerals. Papua New Guinea was one of the few places where these nodules were located in shallow waters instead of deep sea, making it easier to mine. However, even when present in shallow waters, they are still difficult to mine and transport to the surface.

A cyclone forms when a low-pressure area occurs in the ocean

Fact File

Ocean dredging for minerals can have a devastating effect on marine life as the sediments rise up and interfere with photosynthesis.

Oil is extracted from underneath the ocean bed

Oil and Gas Extraction

Crude oil is an essential component that caters to the global fuel supply. Offshore oil and gas exploration has expanded across several areas in the ocean and is going deeper. Water and satellite observations are useful for identifying prospective oil sources underwater. Extracting oil and gas is accompanied by the risk of oil spills and extensive damage to marine life.

OCEAN EXPLORATION

Since ancient times, people have been curious about the ocean depths and the life-forms existing in them. Just until a few decades ago, scientists did not know that any organism could survive 500 metres below the sea. Today, we explore the deep sea through manual expeditions as well as robotic devices.

Underwater Instruments

Neither humans nor robotic devices can remain underwater for a prolonged period for collecting data. Instead, scientists install instruments that collect whale songs, and measurements of temperature, acidity, oxygen and chemical levels. Sensors are attached to buoys that drift to depths of about 1000 metres. Some monitoring devices are also positioned over geologically active seafloors to monitor seismic activity and predict earthquakes.

A diver captures underwater scenes using a specially designed camera

Trenches in the Oceans

Scientists use the term 'deep sea' to describe the regions of the ocean lying below the thermocline. The thermocline is a layer below the influence of the Sun's heating and cooling effects. This part of the ocean is measured as 1000 fathoms (1800 metres).

The deepest parts of oceans are called trenches. An ocean trench is formed when one plate in the crust slides under another. The trenches are deep, dark, cold and experience high pressure. The pressure is about 1000 times higher than at sea level, making it very difficult to explore the ocean depths.

An ocean trench is deep, and under pressure many times higher than on the surface

⚓ Descent of Trieste *into the Mariana Trench*

8th century – The Vikings tried to measure ocean depth using weights attached to ropes.

1521 – Ferdinand Magellan tried measuring the depth of the Pacific Ocean using a 2,400 foot (731 metre) weighted line that did not make it all the way to the bottom.

1623 – The first submarine is built by Cornelius Drebbel.

1818 – Worms and jellyfish living 2000 metres below the surface are caught, providing the evidence for life at such depths.

1865 – The first underwater breathing apparatus is patented.

1872–1876 – The vessel HMS *Challenger* conducts the first formal deep-sea exploration and discovers new species dwelling on the seafloor.

1930 – William Beebe and Otis Barton make history by becoming the first humans to explore the deep sea in a steel bathysphere (a diving device).

1960 – *Trieste* is the first deep sea vessel to descend 10,740 metres into the Challenger Deep, the deepest point in the Mariana Trench.

Fact File

MARIANA TRENCH
The maximum depth is
10,994 metres (36,070 ft)
11°19'N 142°15'E

Japan
China
Taiwan
Vietnam
Philippines
•Northern Mariana Islands
•Guam
•Palau
Federated States
• of Micronesia
Malaysia

The Mariana Trench is so deep that Mount Everest can fit into it and still have about a mile of extra space above!

Robots for Deep Sea Expeditions

The extreme pressure and the other risks for humans at depths make underwater exploration very risky. Even though limited human expeditions occur, findings primarily rely on robots and robotic systems. Remotely operated vehicles (ROVs) are controlled by scientists on board a ship. These ROVs are versatile and capable of different functions. They carry cameras for recording and have manipulator arms as well as containers for collecting samples. Some are also equipped with sonar equipment for accurately identifying depths.

Different from ROVs, autonomous underwater vehicles (AUVs) operate without the need for human controls. They generate maps, measure temperature and chemical levels and take photographs.

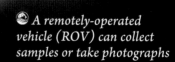
⚓ A remotely-operated vehicle (ROV) can collect samples or take photographs

OCEANS AND CLIMATE CHANGE

Climate change is an important global concern of this century and is closely associated with the oceans. Sea level rise, increasing acidity of the waters and major changes in weather patterns across the world are some of the problems associated with climate change.

Rising sea levels will eventually destroy coastal cities

Burning fossil fuels and releasing carbon dioxide will increase ocean acidity

Ocean as a Buffer

Oceans and climate are closely linked and oceans bear the brunt of climate change. Emission of greenhouse gases has many effects on the oceans, such as:

- Change in water temperature
- Acidification of waters
- Coral bleaching
- Seal level rise
- Coastal erosion and inundation
- Creation of dead zones
- Threat to marine life-forms
- Change in rainfall pattern and seasonal shifts

Humans and Oceans

During the last few centuries, human activity has caused organic carbon, concentrated over millions of years, to be released into the atmosphere. Burning of fossil fuels and other activities has resulted in global warming. If left unchecked, the negative effects on the oceans will continue.

By the end of this century, the sea level will rise significantly, permanently destroying several coastal cities. Coral reefs and several marine flora and fauna are under threat. Polar bears that travel on vast stretches of sea to hunt prey will suffer with the rapidly melting ice in the poles.

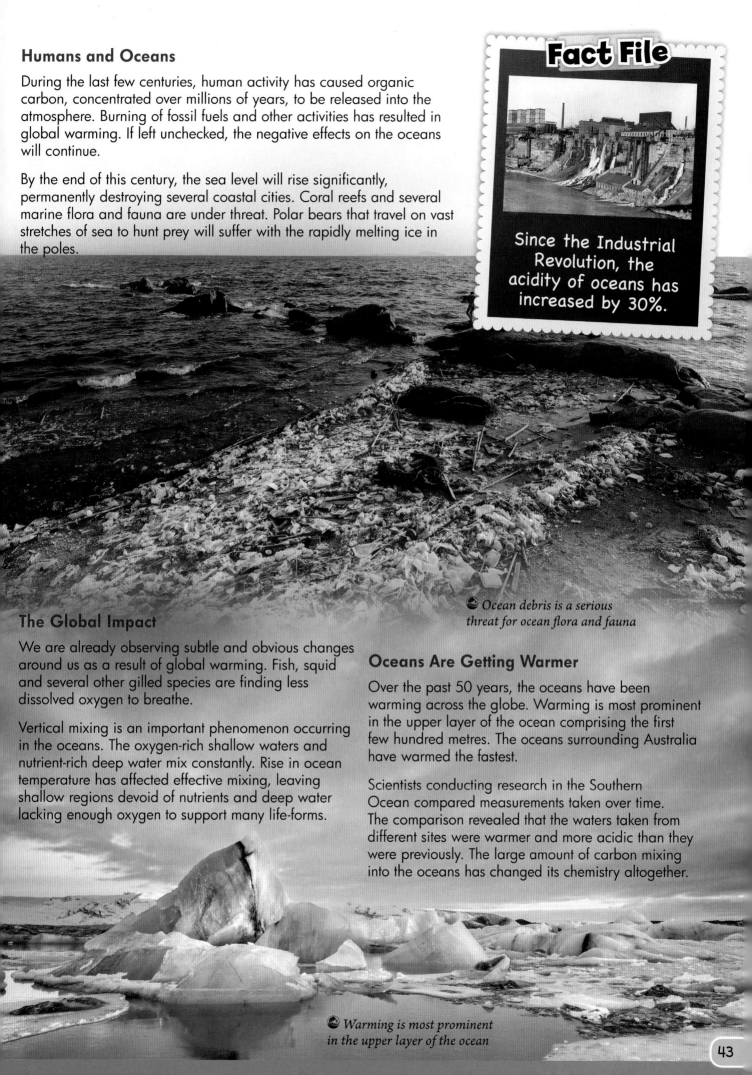

Fact File

Since the Industrial Revolution, the acidity of oceans has increased by 30%.

Ocean debris is a serious threat for ocean flora and fauna

The Global Impact

We are already observing subtle and obvious changes around us as a result of global warming. Fish, squid and several other gilled species are finding less dissolved oxygen to breathe.

Vertical mixing is an important phenomenon occurring in the oceans. The oxygen-rich shallow waters and nutrient-rich deep water mix constantly. Rise in ocean temperature has affected effective mixing, leaving shallow regions devoid of nutrients and deep water lacking enough oxygen to support many life-forms.

Oceans Are Getting Warmer

Over the past 50 years, the oceans have been warming across the globe. Warming is most prominent in the upper layer of the ocean comprising the first few hundred metres. The oceans surrounding Australia have warmed the fastest.

Scientists conducting research in the Southern Ocean compared measurements taken over time. The comparison revealed that the waters taken from different sites were warmer and more acidic than they were previously. The large amount of carbon mixing into the oceans has changed its chemistry altogether.

Warming is most prominent in the upper layer of the ocean

CONSERVATION OF MARINE LIFE

The global conservation of marine life and oceans remains a serious priority for this century. It is essential not only to preserve the ocean's diversity but also to preserve the well-being of all organisms on the planet. Some of the main activities that need reducing include burning of fossil fuels, pollution, overfishing, and habitat destruction.

Early Years of Ocean Conservation

Oceans used to be thought of as vast areas with only a small number of species inhabiting them. This changed with improvement in scuba diving in the 1960s. Since then, divers explored different parts of the ocean, discovering previously unknown spectacular sights and identifying thousands of species residing in the waters. The advent of television and ever-advancing digital technology has helped millions of people learn about, and appreciate, the beauty of the oceans. People were fascinated by the recordings of whale songs. So powerful was the impact that whaling bans slowly began to come into place.

In 1972, the United States passed a law known as the Marine Mammal Protection Act. Ever since, regulations have followed to protect endangered species, prevent overfishing and clean the polluted water of the oceans.

Steller sea lion populations are under threat and have been placed under the Marine Mammal Protection Act

Coral bleaching is a major concern occurring as a result of global warming

Areas of Concern

Marine conservationists focus on several issues plaguing the oceans. Some of the most significant ones include:

- Acidification of oceans
- Warming of ocean waters
- Overfishing and regulation of whaling
- Coral bleaching
- Marine debris
- Endangered marine species
- Oil spills and pollution

The Great Pacific Garbage Patch

Also known as the Pacific trash vortex, this mass of oceanic debris is found in the Pacific Ocean. It extends from the west coast of America to Japan. It is located in the North Pacific Gyre, one of the major gyres in the world. A gyre is a massive system of circulating ocean currents.

The garbage here continuously expands because most of it is plastic litter which cannot biodegrade. Acted upon by sunlight, the plastic breaks down into small pieces. Instead of a floating island of flotsam, the Great Pacific Garbage Patch resembles a cloudy soup of micro-plastics mixed with larger items. The seafloor under the patch is also believed to be a massive underwater trash heap, as nearly 70% of debris sinks down.

80% of the waste enters into the ocean from the shore

North Atlantic Gyre

Great Pacific garbage patch 1,760,000 km²

South Atlantic Gyre

South Pacific Gyre

Indian Ocean Gyre

20% of waste is emitted from ships

The Pacific Garbage Patch is a major global environmental issue

While buying seafood, look for eco labels to certify sustainable fishing

Ways to Help the Ocean

Here are a few ways in which you can contribute to the betterment of the oceans:

1. Reduce energy consumption, use public transportation whenever possible and reduce your carbon footprint.

2. Make conscious choices on the seafood you eat at restaurants or buy in the supermarkets. Encourage sustainable fishing practices whenever possible.

3. Reduce usage of plastic products, use cloth bags for shopping, and buy reusable containers.

4. Avoid buying items such as coral jewellery, or tortoiseshell accessories, that exploit marine life.

5. Volunteer in or support organizations dedicated to preserving and protecting marine environments.

You can volunteer to keep the beaches clean and litter-free

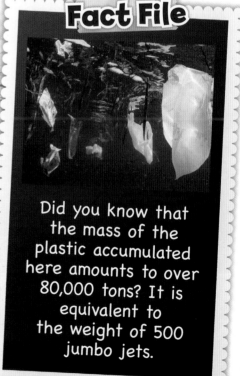

Fact File

Did you know that the mass of the plastic accumulated here amounts to over 80,000 tons? It is equivalent to the weight of 500 jumbo jets.